Born to Run

Hillary A. Hinds

Born to Run

Hillary A. Hinds

Born to Run

Written by Hillary A. Hinds

Copyright© 2022 by Hillary A. Hinds

ISBN: 978-1-990673-03-0

Written by Hillary A. Hinds, Books4dNations Learning Innovations

Cover and book Illustrations by StallionSudio88

Edited by Carlene A. Hurlock

Cataloguing in Publication may be obtained through Library and Archives Canada.

Introduction

Born to Run is a children's picture book by Hillary A. Hinds. The book tells the story of a little boy whose imagination runs free as he sees himself as a runner.

His imagination takes him to various places; however, he doesn't have the legs to run.

This great inspirational story demonstrates the power of imagination and the realization that we can dream of seeing the impossible come to fruition in our lives.

I was born to run. A runner, that's me!

So, of course, I was destined to run.

Even while in my mother's womb, I ran around.

I was born to run. A runner, that's me!

And as I grew, I ran everywhere. You name it; I ran
there too!

Daily I ran through the woods with my dog Fox.
He was my running partner, you see!
These woods were my training grounds as I prepared
for major athletics meets.

I competed in many track and field events in school, always coming out on top.

As I ran many laps around the track, everyone was happy to see me run.

Yes, a runner! That's me. I was born to run.

I was born to captivate the world with my running on the track.

Lifting my hands to appease the crowd after each race.

I traveled to many countries competing in major
athletics events.

I was always on top of my game, as I was never one
to disappoint my fans.

I was a huge influence on the young and old.

Each track meet, they came out to see me run.

A runner, that's me!

Yes, I was born to run.

I competed in many Olympics, taking the gold each
time.

Yes, I was born to run.

I was running a thousand miles and more each week.

A runner, that's me!

I ran all the time, whether it was rainy or sunny.

I was dedicated and determined always to run my

best.

I was born to run.

A runner, that's me!

I have the speed of two cheetahs combined.

A fast runner! That's me.

I was born to run.

Yes, I was born to run. A runner, that's me!

I hope these running shoes will fit one day, but until

that day, I will continue to dream because I was

born to run.

Yes, a runner!

That's me!

Do you not know that those who run in a race all run, but one receives the
prize? Run in such a way that you may obtain it.

1 Corinthians 9:24, NKJV.